Paul Watson is a technology enthusiast and has got massive experience in various technologies like database administration, web application development, automation testing, build automation, continuous integration and deployment technologies. He has worked on most of the technology stacks.

He has hands on experience on UFT, LeanFT, Selenium and Appium. He has used testing frameworks like JUnit, TestNG, Cucumber with Selenium. He has also worked on Struts, Spring, Bootstratp, Angular JS.

His hobbies include travelling to new tourist places, watching basketball, tennis and learning latest technological stuff.

A special note of thanks to my Wife

I would like to dedicate this book to my lovely wife for loving me so much and helping me write this book. Without her support, this book would not have been a reality.

Who this book is for

This book is for automation engineers who want to learn MySQL database management system.

This book will help you master the skills on MySQL.

The book starts with introduction of MySQL and then dives into key concepts as mentioned below.

1. DDL
2. DML
3. DCL
4. Data type and Variables
5. Procedures and Functions
6. Triggers
7. Cursors
8. Transactions
9. MySQL Clients

Table of Contents

1. Introduction

MySQL is a relational database management system. First version of MySQL was released in 1995.

It is developed by David Axmark and Michael Widenius.

It has got below features.

1. Open source and cross platform
2. Used in LAMP and WAMP
3. Many popular applications use MySQL like Wordpress, phpBB, Drupal, Joomla
4. Supports stored procedures, triggers, functions, cursors
5. Supports updatable views
6. Many GUI apps are available for managing MySQL server like MySQL Workbench, phpMyAdmin, Toad
7. We can also manage the server through command line
8. APIs in all major programming languages are available to work with MySQL

2. Installation of MySQL

Official website of MySQL is http://www.mysql.com/

MySQL is offered in various editions as mentioned below.

1. Enterprise Edition
2. Standard Edition
3. Classic Edition
4. Embedded Edition
5. Community Edition

For learning purpose, you should download the community edition.

You can visit https://dev.mysql.com/downloads/file/?id=465371 and download the web installer.

Note that you will have to install python before you start installation process of MySQL.

When installation is completed, MySQL server starts running at port 3306
Default user id is root and password is blank.

MySQL.exe is located in below directory. So you can add this path in PATH environment variable, so that you can use mysql command from the command prompt.

C:\Program Files\MySQL\MySQL Server 5.7\bin

To connect to MySQL from command line, you have to use below command.

```
mysql -u root -p
```

Then you have to press enter key. If you have set the password for root, you will be asked to enter the password. If everything goes well, you will be connected to the mysql.

If you want to use the password in same command, you need to type it right after -p switch without space as shown in below command.

```
mysql -u root -pmypass
```

If you use incorrect password, you may get below error.

```
ERROR 1045 (28000): Access denied for user
'ODBC'@'localhost' (using password: NO)
```

You also get below error if you execute below command.

```
mysql -u root
```

Note that -p switch is very important.

Also do not try to enter the password in the same, otherwise you will get below error.

mysql: [Warning] Using a password on the command line interface can be insecure.

```
ERROR 1045 (28000): Access denied for user
'root'@'localhost' (using password: YES)
```

After the connection is successful, MySQL version is displayed and then you can execute any MySQL command in the interpreter.

To exit MySQL, you have to use exit command.

3. Getting MySQL server information

Once you are connected to MySQL, you can execute help command to view all available commands in MySQL.

To know what all options are supported by show command, you can use below command.
help show

There are many show commands that can give all important information of MySQL server.

For example - You can view all databases as shown in below command.
show databases;

Here is the sample output of above command.

```
| information_schema |
| mysql |
| performance_schema |
| sakila |
| sys |
| world |
```

Information_schema is the database that stores meta data of the user tables, triggers, routines etc.
If you can not see information_schema in workbench, you will have to edit the preferences to show the metadata and internal schemas.

To view which database is currently selected, you can use below command.

```
select database();
```

Above command returns null if no database is selected.
If you execute any command without selecting the database, you will get error saying no Database is selected.

To select the database, you have to use below command.

```
use databaseName;
```

To view all tables in the database, you can use below command.

```
Show tables;
```

To view table schema, you can use below command.

```
Describe tableName;
```

You can use below commands to view procedures

```
SHOW PROCEDURE STATUS;
```

You can use below commands to view functions

```
SHOW FUNCTION STATUS;
```

MySQL supports many storage engines like InnoDB and MyISAM.
To view which storage engine is being used for each table, you need to use below command.

```
SHOW TABLE STATUS;
```

Show table status where name like '%routines%'\G

Note that \G (instead of ; semicolon) is used when you want to display the records in key-value pairs.

information_schema database in MySQL

MySQL stores metadata in the database called as information_schema.
You can view all tables in information_schema using below command.

```
SHOW TABLES;
```

You can use SQL queries to get the information of all tables in MySQL Server.
Below query will return all table and schema names in MySQL Server.

```
SELECT TABLE_SCHEMA, TABLE_NAME FROM
information_schema.tables
```

Below query will return all views and schema names in MySQL Server.

```
SELECT TABLE_SCHEMA, TABLE_NAME FROM
information_schema.tables WHERE TABLE_TYPE
LIKE 'VIEW';
```

Getting server date and time

Below commands can be used to get the current date and time of MySQL server instance.

```
SELECT CURDATE(), CURTIME(), NOW();
```

CURDATE() function displays only date.

CURTIME() function displays only time.

NOW() function displays date as well as time.

Below command shows the name of current user logged into MySQL server.

```
SELECT USER();
```

Below command shows the statistics of the MySQL server like Threads connected, Threads created, read requests, write requests etc.

```
SHOW STATUS;
```

4. RDBMS Concepts

Before we dive into MySQL topics, I want to give you little bit background on what RDBMS exactly means and some of the important concepts related to it.

RDBMS stands for relational database management system. Data is stored in the tables.
Each table has specific number of columns and a set of records. We can retrieve, add, remove, update or delete the records from single or multiple tables using a language called as SQL - Structured Query Language.

Popular relational database management systems

1. Oracle
2. MySQL
3. IBM DB2
4. IBM Informix
5. Microsoft SQL Server
6. Sybase
7. Teradata

Some key concepts to know are mentioned below.

Primary Key - This is the name of the column in a table that helps us identify the unique record in a table. Primary key does not allow null, unique

Foreign Key - This is the name of the column from a table that points to the primary key in another table.

Unique key - data in column can not be duplicated

Referential Integrity - When we have a foreign key in a table and if we try to delete the record pointed by the foreign key in another table, we would not be allowed to do so. This is called as referential integrity.

Candidate key - Minimal set of keys that identify each record uniquely in the table
Non prime attribute - Column that is not a part of candidate key

C1	C2	C3
a1	a2	a3
a1	a2	a4
a2	a4	a5

Find columns that can uniquely identify the records in a table.

```
(C1,C3)  (C2,C3)  (C1,C2,C3)
```

Then find the those sets that do not have proper subset. These are the candidate keys in a table.

```
(C1,C3)  (C2,C3)
```

(C1,C2,C3) has a proper subset. So we will not consider it as a candidate key.

Codd, researcher in RDBMS, had proposed normalization rules for a DBMS.

Normalization helps in data integrity and reduces data redundancy.

List of normalized forms

1. UNF
2. 1NF
3. 2NF
4. 3NF
5. EKNF
6. BCNF
7. 4NF
8. ETNF
9. 5NF
10. 6NF
11. DKNF

A table is in 1NF if it stores atomic (indivisible) values for each attribute (column) in the table and each row in the table is unique.

EMPID	NAME	SKILLS
1	paul	java,php
2	tim	c++

For example in an employee table(with three columns - empid, name, skills), we can have a column with name skills. In that column, we can store multiple skills for each employee(tuple). Data stored in skills column is not atomic, this table does not meet 1NF.

To comply with 1NF, we will have to store the skill values seperately in each row. This will involve creating multiple records for the same employee. This will convert the table in 1NF.

EMPID	NAME	SKILLS
1	paul	java
1	paul	php
2	tim	c++

A table is in 2NF if it is in 1NF and every non-prime attribute of the table is dependent on the whole of every candidate key.

In our employee table, name attribute is a non-prime attribute. But is not dependent on the whole of candidate key(empid and skills columns).

It is dependent upon the empid (subset of candidate key). So this table is not in 2NF.

To get the database in 2NF, we need to split this table in 2 tables as shown below

EMPID	NAME
1	paul
2	tim

A table is in 3NF if The table is in 2NF and each non-prime attribute (column) of table is non-transitively dependent on every key of R.

Consider below table. Here (product name + product version) are candidate keys. Non-prime attribute ManufacturerMainOffice is transitively dependent on candidate key. So this table is not in 3NF.

PRODUCT NAME	PRODUCT_V ERSION	MANUFACT UREDBY	MANUFACTURER MAINOFFICE
S1	1.1	JK	Mumbai
S1	1.2	JK	Mumbai
S3	1.0	BBC	Brisbane

To make the table 3NF compliant, we will need to split it in 2 tables as shown below.

PRODUCTNAME	PRODUCT_VERSION	MANUFACTUREDBY
S1	1.1	JK
S1	1.2	JK
S3	1.0	BBC

MANUFACTUREDBY	MANUFACTURERMAINOFFICE
JK	Mumbai
BBC	Brisbane

A table is considered as normalized if it meets 3NF.
If the table is not normalized, it can lead to update and delete anomaliesER Diagrams are used to design the database schema.

Entity Relationship Model

Each entity is like a table. Each entity has attributes. Attributes can be considered as columns in the database. There are relationships between entities. Relationships between entities can be established using foreign key concept.

In MySQL, we have 3 types of relationships. We can use ER diagrams to show the relationships between different entities.

1. **one to one -** In this relationship, for one record in one table, we have only one record in another table. example - A person holding a passport.
2. **one to many -** In this relationship, for one record in one table, we can have multiple records in another table. example - A customer can have multiple orders
3. **Many to Many -** In this relationship, 3 tables are involved. For one record in one table, we can have multiple records in second table. Also for one record in third table, we can have multiple records in second table. example - 1 or more authors can write a multiple books. To implement the many to many relationship, you should add 3rd table to create the relationship.

All of the above concepts can be better understood with the help of example.

In all our lessons, we would be working with below tables. There is no standard convention to define the table or column names But having consistent naming convention is always better. So we would be using Table names in Capital Letters. Column names would follow PascalCase naming conventions.

We would work on CUSTOMER, ADVERTS and CATEGORY tables.

A **CUSTOMER** table has below mentioned columns.

1. CustomerId - Primary Key
2. FirstName
3. LastName
4. EmailId
5. AddressLine1
6. AddressLine2
7. AreaName
8. AreaCode
9. CityName
10. BirthDate
11. MobileNo
12. Sex

ADVERTS - This is a table containing all advertisements posted by the customers.

1. **AdId -** Primary Key
2. **CustomerId -** Foreign Key pointing to customer record. If we enforce referential integrity, we would not be able to delete the record from the customer table where specific customer has put an advertisement. For each ad, we would be able to find the details of the customer who put that advertisement. Without referential integrity, we could have scenario where there is a record in ADVERTS table but there is no record of the customer in CUSTOMER table who put that ad.
3. AdTitle
4. AdDescription
5. CatId
6. PostedDate

CATEGORY - This is a table containing all categories and sub categories for the advertisements.

1. CatId - Primary Key
2. CatName
3. SubCatName

5. Data Definition Language (DDL)

DDL stands for Data Definition language. DDL is used for defining database schemas.

We can use DDL to perform below operations.

1. Create table
2. Drop table
3. Alter table
4. Rename table
5. Truncate table
6. Enforce referential integrity
7. Specify default values for the columns
8. Specify if column values can have NULL values or not
9. Specify if column values can have only unique values or not
10. Specify data type for each column in a table

5.1 Data types

MySQL supports below types of data types.

1. Numeric Data Type
2. String
3. Date and Time

Numeric data type

bit = single bit

bool and boolean and TINYINT = 1 byte. So you can store signed numbers in the range from -128 to 127. You can store the unsigned numbers in from 0 to 255. If you store 0, it is treated as false. If you store 1, it is treated as true.

SMALLINT = 2 bytes. So you can store signed numbers in the range from -32768 to 32767. You can store the unsigned numbers in from 0 to 65535

MEDIUMINT = 3 bytes. So you can store signed numbers in the range from -8388608 to 8388607. You can store the unsigned numbers in from 0 to 16777215

INT = 4 bytes. So you can store signed numbers in the range from -2147483648 to 2147483647. You can store the unsigned numbers in from 0 to 4294967295

BIGINT = 8 bytes. So you can store signed numbers in the range from -9223372036854775808 to 9223372036854775807. You can store the unsigned numbers in from 0 to 18446744073709551615.

When declaring the Integer data type, we can specify how many characters should be displayed using below syntax.

INT(2) - Number 2 indicates that we need display the value with 2 characters. Application may or may not use this attribute to control the display

Here is a Simple table to understand the data types.

```
CREATE TABLE DATATYPES(
DataId INT(20) UNSIGNED AUTO_INCREMENT
PRIMARY KEY,
Age INT(2) zerofill
);
Insert into DATATYPES (Age) values(4);
```

If we display the record, Age values will be padded with 0. 04

```
FLOAT  -  4 bytes
DOUBLE  -  8 bytes
```

Floating point values are approximate.

DECIMAL - Decimal type can be used in scenarios where you need to preserve exact precision. It is generally used to store financial data as we need a lot of accuracy.

For example DECIMAL(6,2) would be used to store values from -9999.99 to 9999.99.

Here 6 is the precision and 2 is the scale.

Precision means the total number of digits in a number.

Scale means the number of digits to the right of the decimal point in a number.

Float uses 7 digits for precision. Double use 15 digits for precision. Decimal used 28 digits for precision.

SERIAL is an alias for BIGINT UNSIGNED NOT NULL AUTO_INCREMENT UNIQUE.

String data type

CHAR - CHAR data type is used when you know that column value will be of fixed size. For example - Usually states are displayed in 2 character format. So we can use CHAR(2) as a datatype. Also we can store maximum 255 characters with this data type. CHAR is much faster than VARCHAR.

VARCHAR - Main difference between CHAR and VARCHAR is that size is not fixed in VARCHAR. Let us say you want to store the name of the person. We know that length of the name is not fixed. But we also know that Maximum length could be say 100 characters. Then We can use VARCHAR data type like VARCHAR(100). Note that 100 is the max size. If the actual length of the name is say 20 characters then only 20 bytes are used to store the data + 1 or 2 bytes as a prefix to hold length of the actual value. Also we can store upto 65,535 characters with this data type.

BINARY and VARBINARY - These data types are similar to the char and varchar. Only difference is that data is stored in binary format.

```
TINYTEXT - 255 bytes
```

TEXT - 65535 bytes. VARCHAR has a variable max size of 65535 bytes.

```
MEDIUMTEXT - 16,777,215 bytes
LONGTEXT - 4,294,967,295 bytes
```

BLOB stands for binary large objects. We use this data type to store images, audio, video etc.

TINYBLOB, BLOB, MEDIUMBLOB and LONGBLOB are similar to the TINYTEXT, TEXT, MEDIUMTEXT, LONGTEXT. Only difference is that they store the binary data.

ENUM - used to store constant values

Date and Time Data types

DATE - This data type stores only date and displays it in the YYYY-MM-DD format
DATETIME - This data type stores both date and time and displays it in the YYYY-MM-DD HH:MM:SS format
TIME - This data type stores only time and displays it in the format - HH:MM:SS
YEAR - This data type stores only year and display it in the format YYYY

TIMESTAMP - This data type is useful when we want to view data in different time zones. For example, let us say we inserted the record with current timestamp in X time zone. Now if someone tries to view the record in different time zone, he will see the timestamp updated for his time zone.

```
CREATE TABLE TESTTIMESTAMP(
Stamp TIMESTAMP,
DateInserted DATETIME
);

SET time_zone='+00:00';INSERT INTO
TESTTIMESTAMP VALUES(CURRENT_TIMESTAMP,
CURRENT_TIMESTAMP);
```

Now change the time zone and view records.

```
SET time_zone ='+05:00'; select * from
TESTTIMESTAMP;
```

You will notie that timestamp value changes as we change the time zone but date time value does not change even if we change the time zone.

Convert the data type of variables

We can use CAST and CONVERT functions to convert the data type of variables.

```
CAST Function
SELECT (4.5 + CAST('2' AS decimal));

SELECT CONCAT('Converting 4 into string
',CAST(4 AS CHAR));

CONVERT function
SELECT (5 + CONVERT('6', signed int));

SELECT CONCAT('Converting number to
string',CONVERT(1.2,CHAR));
```

Converting charcter sets

```
SELECT CONVERT(_latin1'str1' USING ascii);
SELECT CAST(_latin1'str1' AS CHAR CHARACTER
SET ascii);
```

Converting string to date

```
SELECT STR_TO_DATE('09/01/1986',
'%d/%m/%Y');
```

5.2 Managing Databases

We would be creating a database (Schema) with name "DEALS"

To create a new database, you need to execute below command.

```
CREATE DATABASE DEALS;
```

To select the database, you have to use below command.

```
USE DEALS;
```

To create and select the database in a single command, you can use below syntax.

```
CREATE DATABASE DEALS;USE DEALS;
```

To delete the database, you have to use below command.

```
DROP DATABASE IF EXISTS DEALS;
```

There is no easy command to rename the database. Also depending upon the MySQL engine you are using, renaming process varies.

5.3 Managing Tables

You can create new table using below syntax.

```
CREATE TABLE `customer` (
`CustomerId` bigint(20) unsigned NOT NULL
AUTO_INCREMENT,
`FirstName` varchar(30) NOT NULL,
`LastName` varchar(30) NOT NULL,
`EmailId` varchar(30) NOT NULL,
`AddressLine1` varchar(30) NOT NULL,
`AddressLine2` varchar(30) DEFAULT NULL,
`AreaName` varchar(30) NOT NULL,
`AreaCode` int(30) NOT NULL,
`CityName` varchar(30) NOT NULL,
`BirthDate` date DEFAULT NULL,
`MobileNo` varchar(20) NOT NULL,
`Sex` enum('m','f') NOT NULL,
PRIMARY KEY (`CustomerId`),
UNIQUE KEY `CustomerId` (`CustomerId`),
UNIQUE KEY `EmailId` (`EmailId`)
) ENGINE=InnoDB AUTO_INCREMENT=3 DEFAULT
CHARSET=utf8;
```

SERIAL is an alias for BIGINT UNSIGNED NOT NULL
AUTO_INCREMENT UNIQUE.

```
CREATE TABLE `category` (
`CatId` int(20) unsigned NOT NULL
AUTO_INCREMENT,
`CatName` varchar(30) NOT NULL,
`SubCatName` varchar(30) NOT NULL,
PRIMARY KEY (`CatId`)
) ENGINE=InnoDB AUTO_INCREMENT=2 DEFAULT
CHARSET=utf8;
CREATE TABLE `adverts` (
`AdId` bigint(20) unsigned NOT NULL
AUTO_INCREMENT,
`CustomerId` bigint(20) unsigned NOT NULL,
`AdTitle` varchar(100) NOT NULL,
`AdDescription` varchar(1000) NOT NULL,
`CatId` int(20) unsigned NOT NULL,
`PostedDate` timestamp NOT NULL DEFAULT
CURRENT_TIMESTAMP,
PRIMARY KEY (`AdId`),
UNIQUE KEY `AdId` (`AdId`),
KEY `CustomerId_idx` (`CustomerId`),
KEY `CatId_idx` (`CatId`),
CONSTRAINT `CatId` FOREIGN KEY (`CatId`)
REFERENCES `category` (`CatId`) ON DELETE
NO ACTION ON UPDATE NO ACTION,
CONSTRAINT `CustomerId` FOREIGN KEY
(`CustomerId`) REFERENCES `customer`
(`CustomerId`) ON DELETE NO ACTION ON
UPDATE NO ACTION
) ENGINE=InnoDB AUTO_INCREMENT=3 DEFAULT
CHARSET=utf8;
```

When trying to add a foreign key, you may get generic errno 150 message.

When trying to add foreign key constraint, ensure that below conditions are met.

1. The two tables must have the same charset.
2. Data types of columns being linked should be same.
3. Collation types of columns being linked should be same.
4. Values corresponding to the foreign key column should be available in parent table.

SQL Constraints

1. **Not NULL** - values can not be null
2. **Unique -** values can not be duplicate
3. **Primary Key -** values can not be null and duplicate
4. **Foriegn Key -** For each value for a foreign key column in the child table, there has to be a value in the primary table.
5. **Check -** This is not supported in MySQL
6. Default - We can set the default value for specific column.
7. **Auto Increment** - This constraint means that values for this column will be automatically incremented when new record is inserted.

altering the table

Below query is used to modify the existing column in a table

```
ALTER TABLE Suburb MODIFY COLUMN name
VARCHAR(60);
```

Below query is used to remove existing column from a table

```
ALTER TABLE Suburb DROP COLUMN city;
```

Below query is used to rename existing column from a table

```
ALTER TABLE TEMPTABLE CHANGE Name FirstName
VARCHAR(30);
```

Below query is used to add new column column in a table

```
ALTER TABLE TEMPTABLE ADD LastName
VARCHAR(30);
```

Dropping the table

Let us say you have a table with name SUBURB.

```
CREATE TABLE SUBURB(
id INT(20) UNSIGNED AUTO_INCREMENT PRIMARY
KEY,
city VARCHAR(30) NOT NULL,
code INT(6) NOT NULL,
```

```
name VARCHAR(50)
);
```

We can drop above table using below syntax.
Drop table SUBURB;

Renaming the table

```
RENAME table T1 to T2
```

Please note that if you have any triggers, procedures or functions using old table name, you will have to update them as well.

Truncating the table

If we want to delete all records from the table, you can use below command.
delete from T1;

But above command is time consuming. So we use below command to clear the table.
TRUNCATE TABLE T1;

Difference between delete and truncate

1. Truncate requires the DROP privilege as it drops the table and creats new one with same name.
2. Truncate operation can not be rolled back.
3. Truncate does not invoke ON DELETE triggers.
4. It cannot be performed for InnoDB tables with parent-child foreign key relationships.
5. TRUNCATE is a DDL statement while DELETE is a DML statement.
6. Any AUTO_INCREMENT value is reset to its start value.

Getting table information

You can use below queries to get table information in MySQL.

```
DESCRIBE CUSTOMER;
SHOW COLUMNS FROM CUSTOMER;
```

You can use below command to generate the Create Table SQL query for any table say CUSTOMER.

```
SHOW CREATE TABLE CUSTOMER;
```

A storage engine

A storage engine is used to store the data in table.
You can use below query to view what all engines are available in MySQL server.
show engines;
A MySQL has various types of storage engines as shown below.

1. InnoDB - Supports transactions, row-level locking, foreign keys and save points
2. MEMORY - Used for temporary tables
3. BLACKHOLE - /dev/null storage engine - Nothing is stored.
4. MyISAM - MyISAM storage engine
5. CSV - CSV storage engine
6. ARCHIVE - Archive storage engine
7. PERFORMANCE_SCHEMA - Performance Schema engine
8. FEDERATED - Federated MySQL storage engine

You can check the engine being used by any table using below query.
show table status in Deals where name ='customer';

Below query shows the status of all tables in selected database (schema).
show table status;

Only InnoDB engine supports the transactions. So it is recommended to use this engine.
By default, InnoDB engine is used to create tables.

Collation of a table

Each table in MySQL can have different collation. Each column in a table can have different collation as well.
Collation is nothing but rules applied on the character set encodings.
SQL queries may return different output based on the collation used in the table.

By default, collations are latin1-default collation.

For example - below query will return the records where FirstName contains "AG" or "ag"

```
select * from temptable where FirstName
LIKE "%AG%";
```

To make it case sensitive, you can use COLLATE operator as shown in below query.

```
select * from temptable where FirstName
COLLATE latin1_general_cs LIKE "%AG%";
```

Temporary table

You can create temporary tables using below syntax.
Temporary tables get wiped out as soon as session ends.

```
Create TEMPORARY TABLE xyz(
Id int,
FirstName CHAR(30)
);
```

Cloning the table

You can also clone a table using below syntax. In below
example, we have created new table pqr based on another
table xyz.

```
Create table pqr select * from xyz;
```

To transfer the records from one table into another, you
can use below syntax. Here we have inserted records into
pqr from temptable.

```
Insert into pqr select * from temptable;
```

5.4 Managing Views

Creating view

You can create view as shown in below syntax.

```
CREATE VIEW ADSPERCUSTOMER AS
SELECT
CustomerId, Count(*) TotalAds
FROM
ADVERTS
GROUP by CustomerId
ORDER BY TotalAds DESC;
```

Dropping View

You can use below syntax to drop view

```
DROP VIEW ADSPERCUSTOMER;
```

Getting information on views

To find out which views are available in database, you can use below syntax.

```
SHOW FULL TABLES IN Database_Name WHERE
TABLE_TYPE LIKE 'VIEW';
```

For example, to find out all views in DEALS database, you can use below syntax.

```
SHOW FULL TABLES IN DEALS WHERE TABLE_TYPE
LIKE 'VIEW';
```

Altering views

```
ALTER VIEW ADSPERCUSTOMER AS
SELECT
CustomerId, Count(*) TotalAds
FROM
ADVERTS
GROUP by CustomerId
ORDER BY TotalAds ASC;
```

Renaming views

To rename view, you can use below syntax. Don't get confused by looking at TABLE keyword in below statement.

```
RENAME TABLE ADSPERCUSTOMER to ADSPERCUST
```

6. Data Manipulation Language (DML)

6.1 Inserting records in a table

Consider below table.

```
CREATE TABLE CUSTOMER(
CustomerId SERIAL PRIMARY KEY,
FirstName VARCHAR(30) NOT NULL,
LastName VARCHAR(30) NOT NULL,
EmailId VARCHAR(30) NOT NULL UNIQUE,
AddressLine1 VARCHAR(30) NOT NULL,
AddressLine2 VARCHAR(30),
AreaName VARCHAR(30) NOT NULL,
AreaCode INT(30) NOT NULL,
CityName VARCHAR(30) NOT NULL,
BirthDate DATE,
MobileNo VARCHAR(20) NOT NULL CHECK
(LEN(MobileNo) > 9),
Sex ENUM('m', 'f') NOT NULL
);
```

Below query will insert new record in CUSTOMER table.

```
INSERT INTO CUSTOMER (FirstName, LastName,
EmailId, AddressLine1, AreaName, AreaCode,
CityName, MobileNo, Sex) VALUES (
'Shaun','Tait','Shaun@abc.com','3/4 abc
street','Toowong',4066,
'Brisbane','0138287170','m');
```

```
INSERT INTO CUSTOMER (FirstName, LastName,
EmailId, AddressLine1, AreaName, AreaCode,
CityName, MobileNo, Sex) VALUES (
'Kathy','Tait','Kathy@abc.com','Ascog
street','Taringa',4068,
'Brisbane','0138287171','f');
```

Consider another table.

```
CREATE TABLE CATEGORY(
CatId INT(20) UNSIGNED AUTO_INCREMENT
PRIMARY KEY,
CatName VARCHAR(30) NOT NULL,
SubCatName VARCHAR(30) NOT NULL
);
```

```
INSERT INTO CATEGORY(CatName, SubCatName)
VALUES ('Real Estate','Shared
Accommodation');
```

```
CREATE TABLE ADVERTS(
AdId SERIAL PRIMARY KEY,
CustomerId INT(20) NOT NULL REFERENCES
CUSTOMER(CustomerId),
AdTitle VARCHAR(30) NOT NULL,
AdDescription VARCHAR(1000) NOT NULL,
CatId INT(20) NOT NULL REFERENCES
CATEGORY(CatId),
PostedDate TIMESTAMP DEFAULT
CURRENT_TIMESTAMP
);
```

Alter table modify column AdDescription

```
VARCHAR(1000) NOT NULL;
```

```
INSERT INTO ADVERTS(CustomerId, AdTitle,
AdDescription, CatId) VALUES (1,'Room
available on rent on sharing basis', '
Room is available on rent for very cheap
rate. only $130. Includes all bills -
electricty and internet, fully
furnished.',1);
```

```
INSERT INTO ADVERTS(CustomerId, AdTitle,
AdDescription, CatId) VALUES (1,'Room
available on rent on sharing basis
_Brisbane', 'Room is available on rent for
very cheap rate. only $130. Includes all
bills - electricty and internet, fully
furnished.',1);
```

```
insert into
city(Name,CountryCode,District,Population)
values('Mumbai','IND','Maharashtra',4400000
0);
insert into suburb(Name,code,city)
values('Toowong',4066,'Brisbane');
```

If you execute the query, without specifying the column names, you will get below error.
ERROR 1136 (21S01): Column count doesn't match value count at row 1
You can use below query to get the last insert id in auto increment table.

```
select last_insert_id();
```

When inserting the records in the table that does not have a primary or unique key, duplicate records may be inserted.

To prevent duplicate records, you must have a primary or unique key in your table.

But in case you do not have created a such key, you can still prevent the duplicate records by using 2 queries.

```
insert ignore into Table values(v1,v2)
replace into table values(v1,v2)
```

Consider below table.

```
Create TABLE dup(
LastName CHAR(30),
FirstName CHAR(30)
);
insert into dup values('watson','shaun');
insert into dup values('watson','shaun');
insert into dup values('watson','shaun');
insert into dup values('smith','steve');
```

To see if firstName is repeated, you can use below syntax.

```
select FirstName, count(*) rep from dup
group by FirstName having rep > 1;
```

To remove duplicates, you can use below query.
select FirstName, LastName from dup group by FirstName, LastName;

6.2 Updating records in a table

Below query will update the birth date of the customer having id as 1.
Note that date must be in the yyyymmdd format or yyyy-mm-dd format.

```
UPDATE CUSTOMER SET BirthDate='19860109'
WHERE CustomerId=1;
```

6.3 Deleting records from a table

Below query will delete the record from CUSTOMER table where CustomerId=3

```
delete from CUSTOMER where CustomerId=3
```

To delete all records, you can fire below query.

```
delete from CUSTOMER;
```

6.4 Retrieving Records

Returning all records and all column values using Select keyword.
Below query shows how to get all rows from table

```
CUSTOMER.
SELECT * FROM CUSTOMER
```

Below query shows how to get values from the specific columns from table CUSTOMER.

```
SELECT AreaName, CustomerId FROM CUSTOMER
```

Selecting first 2 records.

```
SELECT * FROM CUSTOMER LIMIT 2
```

Selecting records from the table without repeating a value of a column.
For example - If we execute below query, it will display all area names. The same AreaName may be repeated again in the query.

```
SELECT AreaName FROM CUSTOMER
```

Below query will return only distinct values from AreaName column in CUSTOMER table.

```
SELECT DISTINCT AreaName FROM CUSTOMER
```

Sorting records
Below query shows how to get all rows from table CUSTOMER sorted by FirstName in Ascending order.

```
SELECT * FROM CUSTOMER ORDER BY FirstName
SELECT * FROM CUSTOMER ORDER BY FirstName
ASC
```

Below query shows how to get all rows from table CUSTOMER sorted by FirstName in Descending order.

```
SELECT * FROM CUSTOMER ORDER BY FirstName
DESC
```

We can also sort by multiple columns.

```
SELECT * FROM CUSTOMER ORDER BY FirstName,
LastName DESC;
```

Where Clause - Below query returns the records for male customers only.

```
SELECT * FROM CUSTOMER WHERE Sex='m';
```

We can use other operators like !=, <, <=, >, >= etc. in where clause.
In MySQL, we have 3 logical operators - **AND, OR, NOT.**
AND operator allows you to filter the records matching all column conditions.

```
SELECT * FROM CUSTOMER WHERE Sex='m' AND
LastName='Obama';
```

OR operator allows you to filter the records matching one of the column conditions.

```
SELECT * FROM CUSTOMER WHERE Sex='m' OR
LastName='Obama';
```

NOT operator allows you to filter the records not matching one of the column conditions.
Below query will return all records where customer sex is not male.

```
SELECT * FROM CUSTOMER WHERE NOT Sex='m';
```

You can not use = operator with NULL values. You need to use below syntax to check if value is null.

```
SELECT * FROM CUSTOMER WHERE AddressLine2
IS NULL;
SELECT * FROM CUSTOMER WHERE AddressLine2
IS NOT NULL;
```

LIKE keyword - Selecting the records where values of certain column match the given pattern.
% symbol is used to match zero or more number of characters. For example - in below query, we will get all customer records where last name starts with Ob.

```
SELECT * FROM CUSTOMER WHERE LastName LIKE
'Ob%';
```

Below query will return all records where customer name contains Ob substring.

```
SELECT * FROM CUSTOMER WHERE LastName LIKE
'%Ob%';
```

_ symbol is used to match any one character.
For example - in below query, we will get all customer records where last name starts with Obam and ends with any other letter.

```
SELECT * FROM CUSTOMER WHERE LastName LIKE
'Obam_';
SELECT * FROM CUSTOMER WHERE LastName LIKE
'OBam_';
```

Note that pattern is case in-sensitive. It depends on database server setting. If you want case sensitive filter, you will have to edit the server settings.
Escaping the character using.
Let us say you want to get the records from ADVERTS table where title contains string _Brisbane

```
SELECT * FROM ADVERTS WHERE AdTitle LIKE
'%\_Brisbane%';
```

IN operator allows you to filter the records based on multiple matching values.
Both of the below queries are same.

```
SELECT * FROM CUSTOMER WHERE AreaName IN
('TOOWONG','TARINGA')
SELECT * FROM CUSTOMER WHERE AreaName
='TOOWONG' OR AreaName ='TARINGA')
```

BETWEEN keyword is used to filter the records within specific range.
For example - Below query will return the records from customer table where customer id is in the range from 2-4.

```
SELECT * FROM CUSTOMER WHERE CustomerId
BETWEEN 2 AND 4
```

UNION keyword is used to combine the output of 2 queries.

```
SELECT * FROM CUSTOMER WHERE AreaName
='TOOWONG' UNION SELECT * FROM CUSTOMER
WHERE CustomerId = 2
```

INTERSECT - This keyword is not available in MySQL. You need to use joins to perform INTERSECT like operation in MySQL.

Alias in MySQL

Alias - An alias is a temporary name given to the table or column.
In below example, we have used c as an alias for CUSTOMER table.

```
SELECT * FROM CUSTOMER c where c.CustomerId =2;
```

In below example, we have used c as an alias for CUSTOMER table and Name as an alias for FirstName column.

```
SELECT FirstName Name FROM CUSTOMER c where c.CustomerId =2;
```

Regular expression in MySQL

You can use regular expressions in SQL queries.
For example below query will return the records where LastName starts with b.

```
SELECT * FROM CUSTOMER WHERE LastName REGEXP '^b';
```

Below query will return the records where LastName ends with b.

```
SELECT * FROM CUSTOMER WHERE LastName
REGEXP 'b$';
```

Below query will return the records where LastName contains am.

```
SELECT * FROM CUSTOMER WHERE LastName
REGEXP 'am';
```

We can get the column value in variable using below syntax.

```
Select FirstName into @firstname from
CUSTOMER where CustomerId=1;
```

Joins in SQL Queries

Joins - Joins are used to combine multiple tables and return the results for each record.
There are 3 types of joins.

Inner Join - Gets the records matching in both tables
SELECT column1, column2
FROM table1
INNER JOIN table2
ON table1.column1=table2.column2;

```
SELECT *
FROM CUSTOMER
INNER JOIN ADVERTS
ON customer.CustomerId=adverts.CustomerId
INNER JOIN category
ON adverts.CatId=category.CatId;
```

left (outer) Join - Gets all records from left table as well as matching ones from the right table
SELECT column1, column2
FROM table1
LEFT OUTER JOIN table2
ON table1.column1=table2.column2;

```
SELECT *
FROM CUSTOMER
left outer JOIN ADVERTS
ON customer.CustomerId=adverts.CustomerId;
```

```
SELECT *
FROM CUSTOMER
left JOIN ADVERTS
ON customer.CustomerId=adverts.CustomerId;
```

Right (outer) Join - gets all records from right table as well as matching one from the left table.
SELECT column1, column2
FROM table1
RIGHT OUTER JOIN table2
ON table1.column1=table2.column2;

```
SELECT *
FROM CUSTOMER
right outer JOIN ADVERTS
ON customer.CustomerId=adverts.CustomerId;
```

```
SELECT *
FROM ADVERTS
right JOIN category
ON category.CatId=adverts.CatId;
```

Full Join (outer) - There is no full outer join in MySQL.
Full outer join gets all records from both tables (matching as well as non-matching)
We can simulate the full outer join by firing below query.

```
SELECT column1, column2
FROM table1
LEFT OUTER JOIN table2
ON table1.column1=table2.column2
union
SELECT column1, column2
FROM table1
RIGHT OUTER JOIN table2
ON table1.column1=table2.column2;
```

```
SELECT *
FROM CUSTOMER
left JOIN ADVERTS
ON customer.CustomerId=adverts.CustomerId
Union
SELECT *
FROM CUSTOMER
right outer JOIN ADVERTS
ON customer.CustomerId=adverts.CustomerId;
```

In same way, we can join multiple tables
Joining multiple tables is very easy. Just add another join keyword.

```
SELECT column1, column2, column3
FROM table1
INNER JOIN table2
ON table1.column1=table2.column2
INNER JOIN table3
ON table2.column3=table3.column4;
```

Cross Join - cross join allows you to return all the rows from other table for each row in first table.

```
SELECT *
FROM category
Cross JOIN ADVERTS
```

Subqueries

Subqueries means queries used inside other queries. Main difference between subqueries and joins is that subquery may return scalar value. But Joins always return rows.

```
select * from customer where customerId in
(select custid from oders where
orderdate=now())
```

7. Data Control Language (DCL)

Examples of DCL commands include:
GRANT to allow specified users to perform specified tasks.
REVOKE to cancel previously granted or denied permissions.

Granting and Revoking the privileges

Below is the list of some of the Privileges that you can grant to users.

1. CREATE
2. SELECT
3. DROP
4. DELETE
5. INSERT
6. UPDATE
7. GRANT OPTION

After creating user, you can grant privileges using below syntax.

```
GRANT SELECT ON deals.* TO
'adam'@'localhost';
```

```
FLUSH PRIVILEGES;
```

Note that above privilege will allow adam to only use SQL queries on the tables in deals database.
If user tries to delete, update or insert records in the table, he would get error saying access denied.
To grant all privileges on all database schemas and tables, you can use below syntax.

```
GRANT ALL PRIVILEGES ON *.* TO
'adam'@'localhost';
FLUSH PRIVILEGES;
```

You can check the privileges of any user by executing below command.

```
SHOW GRANTS FOR 'adam'@'localhost'
```

To view grants of current user, execute below query.

```
SHOW GRANTS
```

To Grant File privilege, you need to execute below statements.

```
GRANT FILE ON . to 'adam'@'localhost'
FLUSH PRIVILEGES;
```

8. Variables in MySQL

There are mainly three types of variables in MySQL.

1. User variables (prefixed with @)
2. System Variables (prefixed with @@)
3. Local Variables (No prefix)

Example on User variables are given below.

```
SET @myvar = 1;
select @myvar;
```

Example on System variables are given below.

```
select @@autocommit;
```

We can view all System variables using below syntax.

```
SHOW VARIABLES
SHOW VARIABLES LIKE '%a%';
```

System variables are further categorized in Global and Session. Global variables impact entire server.
While session variables impact only session.

```
SET GLOBAL sort_buffer_size=200000;
SET SESSION sort_buffer_size=200000;
```

Example on Local variables are given below.

```
DECLARE myid INT DEFAULT 0;
```

9. Procedures in MySQL

Procedures are nothing but reusable SQL statements. We can write the SQL statements once in procedure and use the same procedure multiple times with different parameters.

Procedure can take multiple parameters. There are 3 types of parameters in procedures.

1. IN - Input parameter passed by value
2. OUT - Output parameter - This is used to specify that this parameter is going to be returned back
3. INOUT - Input as well as output parameter. This is passed by reference

Below procedure shows that OUT parameter is always NULL by default.

drop procedure if exists TestOutParam;

```
DELIMITER //
CREATE PROCEDURE TestOutParam(out P1
VARCHAR(22))
BEGIN
SELECT P1;
END //
DELIMITER;
SET @V1 = "hello";
CALL TestOutParam(@V1);
```

Main body of the procedure starts with BEGIN keyword and ends with END keyword.

We can declare the variable as shown in below syntax.

```
DECLARE myvariable datatype(size) DEFAULT
defaultValue;
```

```
DECLARE counter INT DEFAULT 0;
```

We can assigne the value to variable using below syntax.

```
SET counter = 2;
```

We can access session and global variables using below syntax.

```
SELECT @mysessionvariabl1;
SELECT @@autocommit;
```

Procedure syntax in MySQL

```
delimiter $$
Create procedure PROCNAME(in param1 int, in
param2 int)
BEGIN
Declare V1 INT;
.....statements
END$$
delimiter ";"
```

Conditional Statements in MySQL

```
IF expression THEN
.....statements;
ELSE
.....statements;
END IF;
IF expression THEN
.....statements;
ELSEIF elseif-expression THEN
.....statements;
ELSE
.....statements;
END IF;
```

Example of conditional statement in MySQL

In below example, we have used If condition to check if the number is odd or even.

```
DROP PROCEDURE IF EXISTS p1;
DELIMITER $$
CREATE PROCEDURE p1 (IN mydata int)
BEGIN
IF (MOD(mydata,2) = 0) THEN
select 'mydata is even';
Else
select 'mydata is odd';
END IF;
END$$
Call p1(11);
SELECT IF(mod(12,2)=0,"Even","odd");
```

Case Statements in MySQL

```
case exp
When ex1 Then
            ..statements
When ex2 Then
            ..statements
Else
            ..statements
End Case
```

```
DELIMITER $$
CREATE PROCEDURE p1 ()
BEGIN
    DECLARE mycase int default 1;
      case mycase
            when 1 then select 'mycase is 1';
            when 2 then select 'mycase is 2';
            when 3 then select 'mycase is 3';
      end case;
END$$
DELIMITER ;
```

Looping Statements in MySQL

There are 3 types of loops in MySQL.
1. While
2. Repeat
3. Loop

```
While (exp) Do
        ..statements
End While;
```

```
Repeat
        ..statements
Until (exp)
End Repeat;
```

```
MyLabel:Loop
      ..statements
End Loop;
```

You can exit the loop using below statement.

```
Leave MyLabel;
```

You can continue the loop (skipping remaining rest of code in a block) using below statement.

```
Iterate MyLabel;
```

Example on loops in MySQL

```
DELIMITER $$
CREATE PROCEDURE p1 (IN mydata int)
BEGIN
DECLARE mycase int default 1;
DECLARE counter int default 5;
MyLabel1:While (counter > 0) Do
select concat('counter is ', CAST(counter
as CHAR(50)));
SET counter = counter -1;
Leave MyLabel1;
End While;
SET counter = 5;
MyLabel2:Repeat
select concat('counter is ', CAST(counter
as CHAR(50)));
Leave MyLabel2;
```

```
Until (exp)
End Repeat;
SET counter = 5;
MyLabel3:Loop
SET counter = counter -1;
IF (counter = 2) THEN
Iterate MyLabel3;
END IF;
select concat('counter is ', CAST(counter
as CHAR(50)));
IF (counter = 0) THEN
Leave MyLabel3;
END IF;
End Loop;
END$$
DELIMITER ;
delimiter ";"
```

```
Create procedure addproc(in a int, in b
int)
BEGIN
    Declare c INT;
   set c=(a+b);
   SELECT concat('addition is ', c);
END$$
delimiter ";"
```

To call procedure you have to use below syntax
call addproc(2,3);
You can get all defined procedures in specific database by
firing below query.

```
SELECT ROUTINE_NAME
FROM INFORMATION_SCHEMA.ROUTINES
WHERE ROUTINE_TYPE='PROCEDURE' AND
ROUTINE_SCHEMA='YOUR_DB_NAME';
```

Adding comments in Procedure

We can add comments in 3 ways.
1. #This is a comment using # symbol
2. -- This is a comment using -- symbol
3. Finally you can add multi-line comment using below syntax.

```
/*
This is a Java style comment
Multi line
*/
```

10. Functions in MySQL

10.1 Built-In functions in MySQL

String Functions

String functions can manipulate a text string

LEFT(string,length) - It is used to get the specified portion of the string from left side.
For example - below query will show only first 3 letters of the name.

SELECT LEFT(FirstName,3) Name FROM CUSTOMER;

RIGHT(string,length) - It is used to get the specified portion of the string from right side.
For example - below query will show only last 3 letters of the name.

SELECT RIGHT(FirstName,3) Name FROM CUSTOMER;

MID(string,start_position,length) - It is used to get the specified portion of the string from any position.
For example - below query will show 3 letters of the name starting at position 2.

SELECT MID(FirstName,2,3) Name FROM CUSTOMER;

LENGTH(string) - It is used to get the length of the string.
For example - below query will show length of the first name of the customer.

```
SELECT LENGTH(FirstName) NameLength FROM
CUSTOMER;
```

LCASE(string) - It is used to convert the string to lower case.

```
SELECT LCASE(FirstName) Name FROM CUSTOMER;
```

UCASE(string) - It is used to convert the string to upper case.

```
SELECT UCASE(FirstName) Name FROM CUSTOMER;
```

REVERSE(string) - It is used to reverse the string.

```
SELECT REVERSE(FirstName) Name FROM CUSTOMER;
```

SUBSTRING(string,position) - It is used to get the SUBSTRING of the string from starting from specific position.
For example - below query will show substring starting at position 2.

```
SELECT SUBSTRING(FirstName,2) Name FROM CUSTOMER;
```

CONCAT(string1,string2,...) - It is used to concatinate the strings together in one string.

```
SELECT CONCAT(FirstName, " " , LastName) Name FROM
CUSTOMER;
```

REPLACE(whole_string,to_be_replaced,replacement) - It is used to replace the portion of the string.
For example - below query will replace Sh by sa in name.
Replacement is case sensitive.

SELECT REPLACE(FirstName,"Sh","sa") Name FROM CUSTOMER;

INSERT(string,start_position,lengthToBeReplaced,newstring) - It is used to insert the substring in another string at specific position.
For example - below query will insert Brett in name starting at position 2 and one letter from original string will be removed at position 2 as well.

SELECT INSERT(FirstName,2,1,"Brett") Name FROM CUSTOMER;

LOCATE(substring,string) - It is used to find the substring in another string. If the substring is found, it's starting position is returned.
If substring is not found, 0 is returned.
For example - below query will find the Sh in First Name.

SELECT LOCATE("Sh",FirstName) Position FROM CUSTOMER;

Numeric Functions

Numeric functions are used to manipulate numbers
FlOOR function returns the nearest integer number that is less than given number

```
SELECT FLOOR(number)
SELECT FLOOR(3.1);
```

Output will be 3.

CEILING function returns the nearest integer number that is larger than given number.

```
SELECT CEILING(number)
SELECT CEILING(4.8);
```

Output will be 5.

ROUND function rounds the number upto given decimals. By default, it rounds the number to 0 decimal places.

```
ROUND(number,[Decimal Places])
SELECT ROUND(12.812,2);
```

Output will be 12.81

```
SELECT ROUND(12.816,2);
```

Output will be 12.82

TRUNCATE function simply truncates the number upto given decimals.

```
TRUNCATE(number,decimal places)
SELECT TRUNCATE(12.812,1);
```

Summarizing Functions

COUNT function returns the total number of records.

```
COUNT(ColumnName)
```

```
select count(*) from CUSTOMER.
```

It will print total number of records from the table CUSTOMER.

AVG function returns the average of all values in a given column.

```
SELECT AVG(ColumnName)
```

MIN function returns the minimum of all values in a given column.

```
MIN(ColumnName)
```

MAX function returns the maximum of all values in a given column.

```
MAX(ColumnName)
```

SUM function returns the sum of all values in a given column.

```
SUM(ColumnName)
```

Functions to manage Null values

COALESCE Function
This function returns first Non-Null value from given parameters.
If there is no non-null value, it returns null.

```
SELECT COALESCE(NULL, NULL, 5);
```

It will return 5.

```
SELECT COALESCE(NULL, NULL, NULL, NULL);
```

It will return NULL.

IFNULL function

If first expression is null, it returns second expression.
If first expression is not null, it returns first expression.
IFNULL(original_value, new_value)

```
SELECT IFNULL(1,4);
```

It will return 1.

```
SELECT IFNULL(NULL,2);
```

It will return 2.

Date and Time Functions

CURDATE method returns current date.

```
SELECT CURDATE();
```

CURTIME method returns current time.

```
SELECT CURTIME();
```

NOW method returns current date as well as time.

```
SELECT NOW();
```

DAYOFMONTH(date) - Returns numeric value of day (1-31)
SELECT

```
DAYOFMONTH(STR_TO_DATE('09/01/1986',
'%d/%m/%Y'));
```

Output will be 09.

DAYOFYEAR(date) - Returns numeric value of day in a year (1-365)

```
SELECT DAYOFYEAR(STR_TO_DATE('09/01/1986',
'%d/%m/%Y'));
```

Output will be 09.

MONTH(date) - Returns numeric value of month (1-12)

```
SELECT MONTH(STR_TO_DATE('09/01/1986',
'%d/%m/%Y'));
```

Output will be 01.

DAYNAME(date) - Returns the name of weekday (sunday, monday etc.)

MONTHNAME(date) - Returns the name of the month (January, Feb etc)

YEAR(date) - Returns Year in 4 digits

HOUR(time) - returns hour in 24 hour format

MINUTE(time) - returns Minutes portion of the time

SECOND(time) - returns seconds portion of the time

DATE_FORMAT() - It is used to format the DATE, DATETIME and TIMESTAMP.

To get the date in dd-mm-yyyy format, use below syntax

```
DATE_FORMAT(NOW(),'%d-%m-%Y')
```

To get the date in dd-mmm-yyyy format, use below syntax

```
DATE_FORMAT(NOW(),'%d-%b-%Y')
```

hour:min:sec format

```
DATE_FORMAT(NOW(),'%h:%i:%s %p')
```

To get the date in 24 hour format, use below syntax

```
DATE_FORMAT(NOW(),'%T')
```

TIME_FORMAT() - It is used to format the TIME, DATETIME and TIMESTAMP.

```
TIME_FORMAT(NOW(),'%h:%i:%s %p')
```

DATE_ADD - It is used to add the interval to given date

```
DATE_ADD(date,INTERVAL expr type)
SELECT DATE_ADD(now(), INTERVAL 5 DAY)
SELECT DATE_ADD(now(), INTERVAL 5 HOUR)
SELECT DATE_ADD(now(), INTERVAL 5 MONTH)
SELECT DATE_ADD(now(), INTERVAL 5 YEAR)
```

DATE_SUB(date,INTERVAL expr type) - It is used to subtract the interval from given date

```
SELECT DATE_SUB(now(), INTERVAL 5 MINUTE)
SELECT DATE_SUB(now(), INTERVAL 5 WEEK)
SELECT DATE_SUB(now(), INTERVAL 5 QUARTER)
```

10.2 User Defined functions in MySQL

Function is just like procedure but only difference is the it returns a value so we can use returned value in SQL queries.

Use below syntax to create a user defined function.

We need to change the delimiter as function would contain multiple statements.

```
delimiter "$$";
```

Do not use reserved keywords as names of functions.

```
delimiter $$
Create function addno(a INT, b INT)
Returns INT Deterministic
BEGIN
        Declare c INT;
        Set c=(a+b);
        Return c;
END$$
delimiter ;
```

Calling a Function

This is how we can call the function.

```
select addno(2,3);
```

Another example on Function

```
USE `deals`;
DROP function IF EXISTS `getCustomerName`;
DELIMITER $$
USE `deals`$$
CREATE FUNCTION `getCustomerName` (id
bigint)
RETURNS VARCHAR(30)
BEGIN
DECLARE tempFirstName VARCHAR(30);
SELECT FirstName INTO tempFirstName FROM
Customer WHERE CustomerId = id;
RETURN COALESCE(tempFirstName, 'Customer
not found');
END$$
DELIMITER ;
```

You can call this function using below syntax.
select getCustomerName(1);

MySQL function to calculate the rectangle area

```
CREATE DEFINER=`root`@`localhost` FUNCTION
`getRectangleArea`(h DOUBLE, w DOUBLE)
RETURNS double
BEGIN
DECLARE area DOUBLE;
SET area = h*w;
RETURN area;
END
```

```
select getrectanglearea(2.1,2.3)
```

Viewing user defined functions

To view user defined functions, you can use below syntax

```
SELECT ROUTINE_NAME
FROM INFORMATION_SCHEMA.ROUTINES
WHERE ROUTINE_TYPE='FUNCTION' AND
ROUTINE_SCHEMA='YOUR_DB_NAME';
```

11. Triggers in MySQL

Triggers are like procedures without parameters. Only difference is that you need to call the procedures explicitly. But triggers get invoked automatically before or after insert/delete/update operation. We can call functions and procedures from within trigger code block. MySQL does not support the CHECK constraints. So you should use TRIGGER.

To view all defined triggers, you can use below syntax.

```
SHOW TRIGGERS;
```

To view triggers from specific database, you can use below syntax.

```
SHOW TRIGGERS FROM YourDatabaseName
```

Example on Trigger

```
delimiter //
CREATE TRIGGER CheckMobileNo BEFORE INSERT
ON CUSTOMER
FOR EACH ROW
BEGIN
          DECLARE errormsg varchar(200);
            IF LENGTH(NEW.MobileNo)< 9
THEN
          SET errorMessage =
CONCAT('MyTriggerError: Invalid MobileNo',
cast(new.MobileNo as char));
signal sqlstate '45000' set message_text =
errorMessage;
          END IF;
END//
delimiter ";"
```

Dropping trigger

To remove tigger, you need to use below syntax.
DROP TRIGGER CheckMobileNo

12. Cursors in MySQL

To work with multiple records, you can use cursors. We can handle each row at a time using cursors.

Key things to know about cursor

1. MySQL cursor is read-only, non-scrollable.
2. MySQL cursor is asensitive. It means that cursor works on actual table data. If any other user changes the data, those changes are reflected in the cursor as well.

Creating a new cursor in MySQL

Declare the cursor using below syntax. The cursor declaration shoud be done after other variables are declared.

```
DECLARE mycursor CURSOR FOR
SELECT_statement;
```

Then open the cursor using below syntax.
OPEN mycursor;

Fetch one row at a time using below syntax.

```
FETCH mycursor INTO v1, v2;
```

At the end, you need to close the cursor using below syntax.

```
CLOSE mycursor;
```

When you try to fetch the rows from the empty cursor, you get an error. So to handle this error, we need to define NOT FOUND handler using below syntax.

```
DECLARE CONTINUE HANDLER FOR NOT FOUND
SET completed = 1;
```

Example on the cursor

```
DELIMITER $$
CREATE PROCEDURE getCustdata (INOUT data
varchar(1000))
BEGIN
DECLARE completed INTEGER DEFAULT 0;
DECLARE tempdata varchar(50) DEFAULT "";
DEClARE mycursor CURSOR FOR
SELECT FirstName FROM CUSTOMER;
DECLARE CONTINUE HANDLER FOR NOT FOUND
SET completed = 1;
OPEN mycursor;
myloop: LOOP
FETCH mycursor INTO tempdata;
IF completed = 1 THEN
LEAVE myloop;
END IF;
SET data = CONCAT(tempdata,";",data );
END LOOP myloop;
CLOSE mycursor;
END$$
DELIMITER ;
```

You can test your cursor using below statements.

```
SET @custdata = "";
CALL getCustdata(@custdata);
SELECT @custdata;
```

13. Transaction control

A transaction is nothing but sequence of SQL statements executed as a one unit.
A transaction should meet ACID properties.

By default, each sql statement is considered as a transaction. So as soon as you execute the SQL statement, changes are committed to the database.
There is a variable with name autocommit that controls this behaviour.

You can use below query to view if autocommit is on or off.

show variables where Variable_name = 'autocommit'

You can turn on or off autocommit by using below syntax.

```
set autocommit = 0
```

Example of MySQL transaction

At the end of below transaction, all changes will be committed and customer table will be updated.

```
start transaction;
update customer set FirstName='Shaun' where
CustomerId=1;
update customer set FirstName='Fredrick'
where CustomerId=2;
commit;
```

At the end of below transaction, all changes will be rolled back and customer table will remain as it was before the transaction was started.

```
start transaction;
update customer set FirstName='Shaun1'
where CustomerId=1;
update customer set FirstName='Fredrick1'
where CustomerId=2;
rollback;
```

14. Event scheduler

Events are used to execute some SQL code at specified time just like windows scheduler or cron jobs in Linux.

Here are the steps to create events.

1. Start the scheduler
2. Create Event
3. View the active events from the database.

To start the event scheduler process, you need to update the event_scheduler variable to ON.

```
SET GLOBAL event_scheduler = ON;
```

Once you do that, you will see that event_scheduler process is started using below statement.

```
SHOW PROCESSLIST;
```

Next you need to create the event as shown in below example. Here we are first dropping the event and then creating new one with name MyEvent.
This event starts now and ends after 1 minute repeating each 15 seconds. After every 15 seconds, it will insert a record in Table - dup.

```
Drop event if exists MyEvent;

CREATE EVENT MyEvent
ON SCHEDULE EVERY 15 second
STARTS now()
ENDS now() + INTERVAL 1 minute
DO
```

```
INSERT INTO dup VALUES('Testing
Event',now());
```

You can view all active events using below query.

```
SHOW EVENTS FROM Deals;
```

In case, your events are not working as expected, ensure that event_scheduler is ON. You can also check the server logs for any errors.

15. Tuning MySQL Server Performance

Indexing is used to speed up the performance of the database.

We can create an index on a specific column in a table containing huge number of rows.

To view what index is being used on the table, you can use below syntax.

```
SHOW INDEX FROM CUSTOMER
show index in customer;
```

You can create 3 types of index.
1. Unique Index
2. Normal Index
3. FullText Index

```
CREATE UNIQUE INDEX `idin` on `temptable`
(`Id`);
CREATE INDEX `name` on `temptable`
(`FirstName`);
ALTER TABLE `temptable` ADD INDEX `name`
(`FirstName`);
ALTER TABLE `temptable` DROP INDEX `name`;
ALTER TABLE `temptable` Add FULLTEXT
lname(`LastName`);
```

Preventing performance issues due to SQL attacks

To prevent SQL injection, you need to do below things.

1. Escape special SQL characters from the input values used in the query.
2. Use prepared statements.

16. MySQL Administration

16.1 Managing users

Creating new Users

```
CREATE USER 'adam'@'localhost'
IDENTIFIED BY 'passwd'
```

User Roles

You can assign the role to user using MySQL workbench UI. There is no sql statement to assign specific role to the user.

Deleting users in MySQL

To remove the user, you can use below syntax.

```
DROP USER 'adam1'@'localhost';
```

16.2 Importing and Exporting data

Exporting database/ Taking back up

```
mysqldump.exe –e –uroot -p**** -hlocalhost
DEALS > "C:\Users\db1.sql"
mysqldump.exe –e –uroot -p**** -hlocalhost
DEALS > "C:\Users\MySQL\db1.sql"
```

To dump the data from any query into the file, you can use below syntax.

```
select * from dup into OUTFILE
'c:\\abc.txt';
```

Note that the file should not exist there before executing the query. If the file is already there, you will get error saying can not overwrite, file already exists.

To run above query, you should have File creation privilege.
You can check the privileges of any user by executing below command.

```
SHOW GRANTS FOR 'adam'@'localhost'
```

To Grant File privilege, you need to execute below statements.

```
GRANT FILE ON . to 'adam'@'localhost'
FLUSH PRIVILEGES;
```

If the server is running with --secure-file-priv option, you will not able to execute above query. To disable secure-file-priv option, you will have to comment this in my.ini file.

You can also specify the format of the output file as shown below.

```
select * from dup into OUTFILE
'c:\\abc.txt'
Fields terminated by ',' enclosed by '"'
lines terminated by '\r\n';
```

You can view the file path by executing below query

```
SHOW VARIABLES LIKE 'secure_file_priv';
```

Importing database

```
mysql –u[user name] -p[password] -
h[hostname] [database name] <
C:\[filename].sql
```

You can also use mysqlinput tool to import the data.

Another way to load data in a table is by using LOAD command.

```
LOAD DATA LOCAL INFILE 'c:\\abc.txt' into
dup;
```

You can also specify the format of the data being loaded.

```
LOAD DATA LOCAL INFILE 'c:\\abc.txt' into
table dup
Fields terminated by ',' enclosed by '"'
lines terminated by '\r\n';
```

17. Database Testing

It is very important to perform complete database testing.

You can test below things while doing database testing.

1. Data Mapping - We can verify that data entered in application UI is properly being saved in correct columns.
2. We can also test that CRUD (Create, Retrieve, Update, Delete) actions are working correctly.
3. We can also test ACID properties of database.
4. We can also test Data Integrity.
5. We can also test Business Rules.

Database testing also involves testing below things.

1. Verification of default values, unique value constraints.
2. Verification of triggers
3. Verification of procedures and functions.
4. Verification of queries involving NULL values.
5. Verification of Referential Integrity.
6. Verification of the user roles and privileges.
7. Verification of transactions Rollbacks and savepoints.

18. MySQL Clients

18.1 Workbench

Workbench allows you to manage your MySQL database very easily through GUI.

You can do all database operations in MySQL workbench.

Sometimes, Workbench does not show the information_schema database. So you have to edit the preferences to show these metadata schemas.

To edit the schema, table or triggers, you need to right click on table name and then click on Alter Table.

18.2 PHPMyAdmin

PHPMyAdmin is a web app that allows managing your MySQL databases very easily.

When you install WAMP or LAMP, PHPMyAdmin is also installed.